GROSS AND Frightening ANIMAL FACTS

SCARY ANIMALS

Stella Tarakson

MASON CREST

THAT'S SCARY!

Mason Crest
450 Parkway Drive, Suite D
Broomall, Pennsylvania 19008
(866) MCP-BOOK (toll free)

First printing
9 8 7 6 5 4 3 2 1

ISBN (hardback) 978-1-4222-3928-5
ISBN (series) 978-1-4222-3923-0
ISBN (ebook) 978-1-4222-7865-9

Cataloging-in-Publication Data on file with the Library of Congress

Scary Animals
Text copyright © 2015 Pascal Press Written by Stella Tarakson

First published 2015 by Pascal Press PO Box 250, Glebe, NSW 2037 Australia

Publisher: Lynn Dickinson Principal Photographer: Steve Parish © Nature-Connect Pty Ltd
Additional Photography: See p. 48 Researcher: Clare Thomson, Wild Card Media Editor: Vanessa Barker

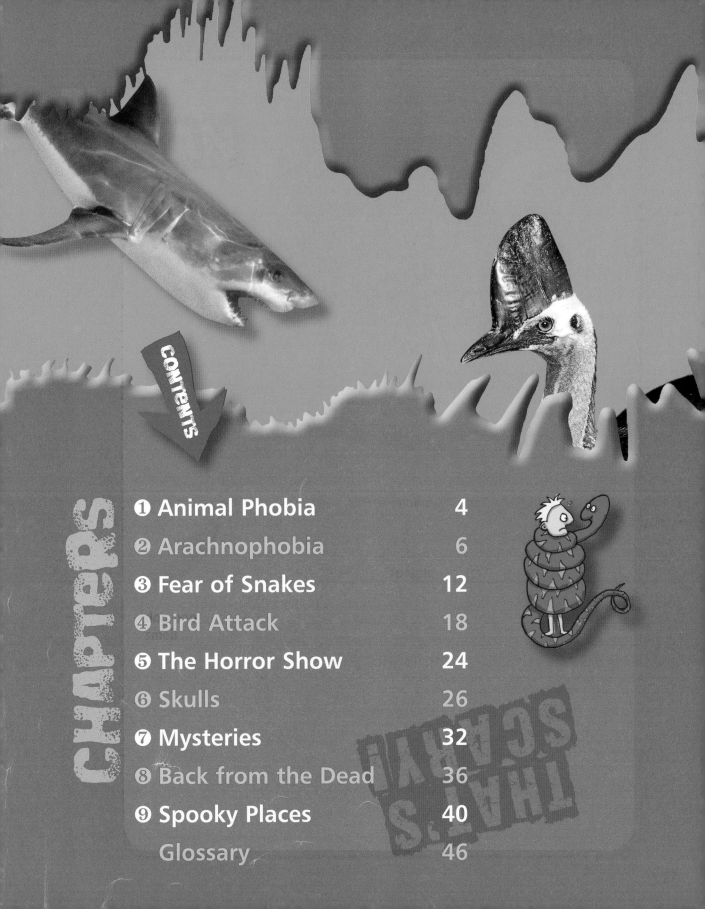

CONTENTS

CHAPTERS

THAT'S SCARY!

CHAPTER 1

ANIMAL PHOBIA

A phobia is an extreme fear totally out of proportion to the danger—so much so, it can interfere with the sufferer's daily life. Some people even refuse to leave their houses! Common phobias include fear of heights, open spaces, confined spaces and certain animals.

It's normal to get scared when you see something dangerous—it's your brain telling you to watch out!

YOU SHOULD SEE MY BROTHER!

A face you don't want to meet in the dark—the black wolf-fish

SURVIVAL OF THE SPECIES

Lots of people have phobias when it comes to snakes and spiders. But not many are frightened of flowers! That's because we're geared to fear things that threatened our ancient ancestors, way back when humans were evolving. That's also why it's less common to have phobias about modern-day threats, such as classroom phobia!

Maori octopus

FIGHT THE FEAR

Most animals are more afraid of us than we are of them. They might act aggressively by baring their teeth, but it's often an attempt to scare us off. If you leave them alone, they'll probably leave you alone too!

AARGH! A HUMAN!

Vespertilio murinus

CHAPTER 2

ARACHNOPHOBIA

They scuttle. They jump. They pounce. No wonder so many people are scared of spiders! The extreme fear of these creepy crawlies is known as "arachnophobia." The humble huntsman spider, however, has an unfair reputation. They're a familiar sight in cars and homes and have sent many people screaming—maybe even your dad! Luckily, huntsman spiders aren't aggressive. Even so, keep your distance. Their bites aren't lethal, but they're certainly painful!

WHAT ROT!

It's a myth that white-tailed spider bites make flesh rot!

SUPER SILK

Spiders make silk from glands in their bottoms. It comes out as a liquid through their spinnerets, and spiders use it to build their webs. If you've ever walked into a spiderweb, you'll know they are amazingly strong and stretchy! The silk is used to catch prey, to attract mates and to hold eggs.

WOW! THAT SPIDER CAUGHT A BIG ONE!

Funnel-web spider

FATAL FANGS

Only two Australian spider species, the red-back and the Sydney funnel-web, are deadly. The funnel-web is aggressive and is one of the most dangerous spiders in the world. A bite is considered a medical emergency. Since antivenom was introduced, however, there have been hardly any deaths from spider bites.

Wolf spider with
captured fly

HELP ME!

ALL THE BETTER TO SEE YOU WITH

Are you scared of the wolf spider's beady little eyes? Don't be—because they've got beady BIG eyes! Despite having up to eight eyes, most spiders have poor vision. They rely on other senses to locate prey. But wolf spiders have great eyesight, even in dim light. The four largest of their eight eyes help them to recognize the movement of their prey. Wolf spiders are easy to spot at night because their big eyes shine brightly in a flashlight beam. It's enough to make anyone howl at the moon …

SUCK IT UP

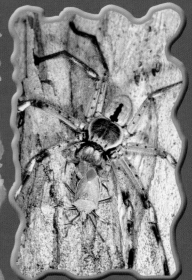

Spiders can't chew — they can only swallow liquids. They inject their prey with a fluid that turns it into mush, and then the spiders suck up the gooey insides. It's just like drinking through a straw!

NEXT MEAL?

DARLING, THERE'S NOTHING TO EAT FOR LUNCH!

Love can be lethal for spiders, with males often much smaller than females. This male golden orb spider is only 0.2 inches (6 millimeters) long—the female is five times its size! So unless the female has already eaten, she just might make a snack out of her tiny male companion!

BUG GUTS SMOOTHIE. MY FAVORITE!

WINGING IT

You'll never guess what bird-eating spiders eat—birds! These amazing spiders catch them and crush them with their powerful jaws.

MOMMY, CAN I HAVE THE WINGS?

I'M A WEB DESIGNER!

BAT-MUNCHING SPIDERS

Did you know there are spiders that eat bats? Such spiders can be found on every continent except Antarctica. In Australia, there are giant golden orb-weaving spiders. Not surprisingly, these spiders are huge—with a leg span of up to 4—6 inches (10–15 centimeters) across. Their webs are more than 3 feet (1 meter) wide. Big enough to catch Batman!

SPIDER-MUNCHING BATS

Some bats like to return the favor. Golden-tipped bats are fond of munching on web-building spiders. The bat's broad wings allow them to hover and snatch spiders straight form their webs.

DINNER TIME

COME INTO MY PARLOR

Golden orb-weaving spiders usually eat insects—such as flies, beetles and cicadas. But sometimes their strong webs trap small bats or birds, like this zebra finch. The spider will then indulge in a super-sized feast!

CHAPTER 3

FEAR OF SNAKES

Throughout time, different cultures have used snakes as symbols of evil. They are featured as the bad guys in myths, legends and even modern stories—and it's not surprising. Snakes slither. They slide. They hiss. They move without legs and have expressionless reptilian faces. The excessive fear of snakes is known as "ophidiophobia," and it's one of the most common phobias in the world.

the GRANDADDY of them all

Snakes have been around much longer than humans—and some used to be monster sized! The gigantic Titanoboa weighed over a ton and measured a whopping 2,205 lbs. (1 ton). Fortunately for us, it existed 58 million years ago. Like modern-day pythons and boas, the Titanoboa killed its prey by squeezing it. You wouldn't want to see one of these slithering around your backyard!

A BAD RAP

Less than a quarter of all snakes are venomous. They rarely attack unless provoked. To be on the safe side, keep your distance and give these creatures the respect they deserve!

HARD TO SWALLOW

Some snakes have been known to swallow humans! The reticulated python of Southeast Asia is the world's largest snake. It's about 33 feet (10 meters) long and has, on rare occasions, even lunched on people!

A HYPNOTIZING SIGHT

> FANGS FOR NOTHING!

It looks like an amazing trick—a snake being hypnotized with pipe music. Snake charmers were once a common sight in India. The snakes would rise up and appear to weave and sway to the tune. Actually, the snakes were just responding to the pipe, which they considered a threat. Many of these snakes had their fangs removed to stop them from hurting their handlers—not exactly fair for the poor snake!

> I GOT THEM AT THE VAMPIRE SHOP!

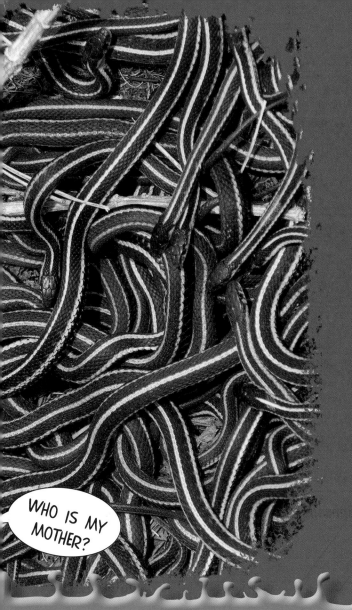

WHO IS MY MOTHER?

CONCENTRATE

How would you like to step into a den filled with 25,000 snakes? In Canada, red-sided garter snakes hibernate over winter to escape the cold. A single den is around the size of an average living room. But instead of wall-to-wall carpet, you'd find wall-to-wall snakes! These dens are the largest concentration of snakes anywhere in the world.

ADDERS MULTIPLY

Fortunately, such huge groups of snakes are not everywhere. However, when they do get together to breed, adders rarely exceed groups of more than 30.

THE SNAKE FILES

Arafura file snakes might look scary, but roasted on hot coals they make a tasty treat! Indigenous Australians hunt for these snakes under logs submerged in riverbanks. But don't worry—the snakes aren't venomous!

Yes, this girl is smiling! That's because the olive python is nonvenomous and harmless to humans. It mainly eats small mammals, birds, reptiles and frogs. It kills its prey by suffocation—or cuddling them to death! Sadly, olive pythons are sometimes mistaken for the venomous king brown snake and are killed unnecessarily.

GIVE ME A HUG

I'LL GO DOWN IN HISSSSSSTORY!

ISLAND
MONSTERS

You might think 3-foot (1-meter)-long snakes are scary, but that's nothing compared to their island cousins! Some islands are home to giant tiger snakes, which are much longer than their mainland relatives. On Carnac Island, off the coast of Perth, tiger snakes grow up to 7 feet (2 meters) in length. And on Chappell Island, near Tasmania, they can grow as long as 8 feet (2.4 meters)! Keep in mind that the average height for men in is less than 6 feet (180 centimeters)!

SKINNED
ALIVE

It sounds like a scene from a horror movie. Skin peels back from a creature's head, down over the rest of its body, and then a snake slithers out! This is actually what snakes do when a new skin has formed beneath their old skin. The old skin is sloughed off, turning inside out like a discarded sock. It usually takes a few hours to shed a skin.

CHAPTER 4

BIRD ATTACK

For ornithophobia sufferers, just being swooped by a bird is a terrifying experience. But being attacked by a whole flock at once is their worst nightmare! That's exactly what happened to the unfortunate residents of a town in California, USA, one summer back in 1961. Hundreds of usually nonviolent seabirds suddenly began diving at people, buildings and moving cars for no apparent reason. The crazed attacks then ended as mysteriously as they began. Scientists now believe that the birds were driven crazy by poisoned plankton containing toxins that damaged their brains. The events even inspired famous director Alfred Hitchcock's thriller film *The Birds*.

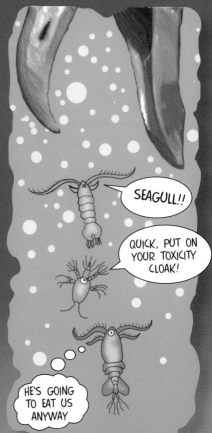

SEAGULL!!

QUICK, PUT ON YOUR TOXICITY CLOAK!

HE'S GOING TO EAT US ANYWAY

STUPID PLANKTON!

AHHHHHH HHHHHH!

Although many of the swooping bird effects were done in the studio, the actress in *The Birds* had real birds attached to her face with wire, making the birds panic. Her screams were for real!

DEATH BY BIRD

Cassowaries and ostriches are two birds with a lot in common. They're both huge — the ostrich is the largest living bird in the world — and they both can't fly. These formidable fowl are also the only birds in the world that have killed humans by attacking them. They can cause serious injury with their vicious claws and by kicking with their strong legs. The best advice when it comes to encountering these birds in the wild? Keep your distance! The only known person to die from a cassowary attack was trying to kill the bird.

HE STARTED IT!

HURRY UP, I CAN'T WAIT ALL DAY!

THE VULTURE STRIP

Vultures are scavengers and don't usually attack and kill their prey. They prefer to eat carrion, which is the dead and decaying flesh of animals. However, vultures have been known to attack newborn or wounded animals. Shooting squads were even used to protect injured soldiers from vultures during the Crimean War of 1854. A vulture's strong and powerful beak can easily rip through decaying flesh. It takes just 20 minutes for a vulture to strip a small animal, such as a rabbit, down to the bone!

COMMON SWOOPERS

I AM ONE ANGRY BIRD!

Magpies: About 10 percent of magpies swoop aggressively to protect their young. Most swoopers are male.

Butcherbirds: Butcherbirds have a formidable beak and may have a go at you if you get too close.

Masked lapwings or plovers: From July to November, these masked avengers swoop to protect their young.

Red wattlebirds: They're unlikely to attack, but they'll certainly snap their beaks and try to frighten you off.

Willie wagtails: These tiny birds can be surprisingly aggressive, even pecking at your head!

Noisy miners: Pet dogs and cats are often the victims of targeted mobbing campaigns.

Kookaburras: Kookaburras have even been known to steal sausages from barbecues!

Gulls: Gulls often dive-bomb people having picnics at the beach. Hold on tight to your hot dogs.

MAGPIE SWOOP FACTS

- About 10 percent of magpies swoop at humans.
- Nearly all the swooping is done by males.
- Around half will only swoop at people who pass on foot.
- Fewer than 1 in 10 will only swoop at cyclists.
- Most attacks occur August to November, when chicks are still in the nest.
- Around 85 percent of those who live near magpies have been swooped at some time in their lives.
- Sometimes individuals are targeted, while their friends and family are left alone.

DEFENSE STRATEGIES

Maybe these work and maybe they don't — but they're worth a try!

- traveling with other people
- facing the bird as you walk past
- holding up an umbrella or stick
- putting false eyes on the back of a cap so the bird thinks you're watching it
- threading long cable ties through a bike helmet
- trying to befriend the bird with food
- avoid the nesting area if possible

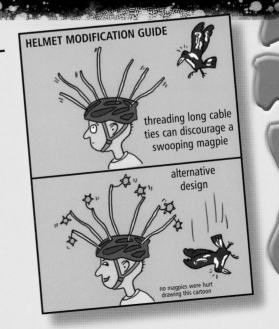

HELMET MODIFICATION GUIDE

threading long cable ties can discourage a swooping magpie

alternative design

no magpies were hurt drawing this cartoon

CREEPY RAVEN ROOSTS

Like something from a horror film, up to 1,000 ravens roost together at night. It might seem creepy, but it's actually a form of self-protection. It also allows the birds to share information about where food can be found.

SPREADING THE WORD

Crows in Brisbane were found to have 316 different calls. That's quite a vocabulary! Like dolphins and apes, crows can "talk" to each other. And it seems they are masters of communication. Crows in Brisbane took two decades to learn how to eat cane toads safely. But when the toads migrated to Darwin, the crows there immediately knew what to do. Maybe they'd been told?

ANOTHER ROADSIDE CAFÉ

Crows have a reputation for being evil and are often used to freak people out in horror movies. But they're actually incredibly smart birds, doing what comes naturally. That means cleaning up roadkill — much better than us having to do it!

CHAPTER 5

THE HORROR SHOW

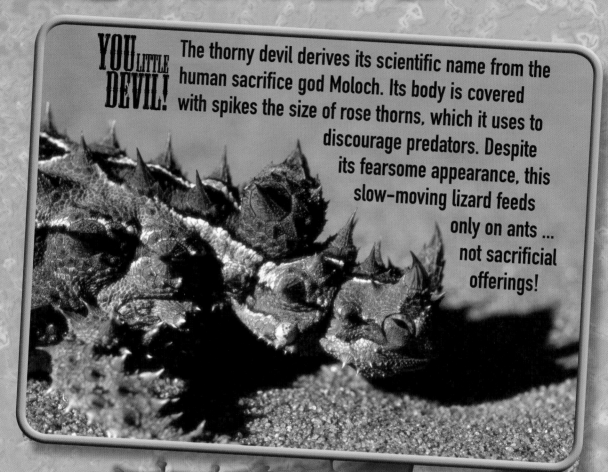

YOU LITTLE DEVIL! The thorny devil derives its scientific name from the human sacrifice god Moloch. Its body is covered with spikes the size of rose thorns, which it uses to discourage predators. Despite its fearsome appearance, this slow-moving lizard feeds only on ants ... not sacrificial offerings!

BLOOD-SQUIRTING EYEBALLS

AND MY NEXT TRICK IS...

The horned lizards of North America have a gory defense mechanism—and it comes out of their eyeballs! By constricting the blood vessels around their eyes, they can shoot a foul-smelling squirt of blood at a predator up to 5 feet (1.5 meters) away.

SCORPION SURPRISE

Finally, an Australian animal that's less deadly than its overseas relatives! There are 43 species of scorpions in Australia, and even though all can sting—some very painfully—none are highly venomous. Some scorpion species found elsewhere in the world are lethal and kill hundreds of people a year.

CENTIPEDE STAMPEDE

Despite reports that a centipede once killed a dog, these creepy crawlies don't pack enough poison in their claws to kill a human, even though it is painful! Their name is also a bit of a contradiction. "Centi" means 100 and "pede" means feet, but centipedes don't actually have 100 feet. The number varies and can range from 15 to 191 pairs.

DRAT, LOST ANOTHER SHOE!

CHAPTER 6

SKULLS

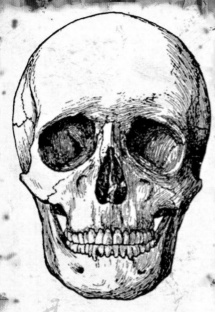

FIG. 8
Front view of the skull

Nothing says death more than a skull—that ghastly grin, those hollow eyes, the blank stare. If you see a picture of a skull anywhere—on a bottle, on a door, even in a computer game—the message is clear. Beware! Death and danger lie ahead!

NOBODY LOVES ME.

SKULLS IN THE CLOSET!

One odd Englishman has a very unusual collection — animal skulls! The amateur taxidermist started collecting skulls in his teens and has now filled two rooms of his house with his hobby. His collection of over 2,000 creature craniums includes a bat, newt, giraffe and cuckoo. He even has the skull of a two-headed cow!

I'VE LOST MY HEAD!

ALL SHAPES AND SIZES

Eastern cave bat

Flying fox

Spoonbill bird

Crocodile

INCISIVE INCISORS

An extinct giant wombat (*diprotodon*).
My, what big teeth you had! All the
better to eat roots and grass.

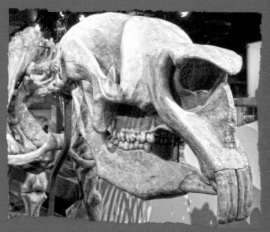

LAST SUPPER

Skulls and skeletons are often
all that's left of dead animals
after scavengers have been
at them. You can identify
animals from their skulls and
can often tell if they were
vegetarians or meat eaters by
looking at the size and shape
of their teeth and jaws.

FEROCIOUS FACE-OFF

Scientists have made 3-D models of the skulls of various animals — then pitted them together in a face-off, to see whose bite is the most powerful.

WINNERS ARE GRINNERS!

HAVING A BIG BITE GIVES YOU DISTINCTION, BUT IT DOES NOT SAVE YOU FROM EXTINCTION.

BITE FORCE in Newtons

T-Rex (extinct)	35,000–57,000 N	(39–64 x human bite force)
Great White Shark	17,790 N	(19 x human bite force)
Crocodile	16,460 N	(18 x human bite force)
Hyena, Tiger, Lion	4,450 N	(5 x human bite force)
Human	890 N	

I DON'T EAT APPLES!

WATCH THE CROC CRUSH THIS APPLE!

JAWSOME!

So how do researchers measure bite force? In the case of crocodiles, they strap the animal down, place a measuring device between its back teeth—and stand back. Researchers have said a croc's bite is so powerful it sounds like a gunshot!

Open your mouth wide . . . wider . . . wider . . . and close it again. Where do you think your bite force was strongest? For mammals, the bite force weakens as the jaw opens wider. But for some animals like the shark, the wider the jaws are opened, the more forceful its bite.

OPEN WIDE

SPACE-LIZARD

The Komodo dragon has strong neck muscles and 60 razor-sharp teeth, which make this giant lizard a powerful opponent. It also has what researchers call a "space-frame" skull. Though incredibly light, the skull's interlocking structure can handle very large loads.

HYENA vs TASMANIAN DEVIL

The hyena is often called the world's most vicious biter, but researchers disagree. They claim the Tasmanian devil has the most powerful bite, once you consider its relatively small body weight. A dog would have to be three times a devil's weight just to match the strength of its bite. A a 13-lb. (6-kilogram) devil can even kill a 60-lb. (30-kilogram) wombat! Who's laughing now?

WHY DID THE WOMBAT DIE?

BECAUSE I ATE IT!

MARSUPIAL LION vs AFRICAN LION

Everyone knows the lion is the king of the jungle, but have you ever heard of the king of the outback? No? That's probably because it's been extinct for the last 30,000 years! If it were alive, the Australian marsupial lion would be so strong it could even take down the African lion. It's still considered the most powerful biter of its size among all mammals, living or extinct!

© Queensland Museum, Robert Allen

RUMBLE
IN THE FARMYARD

Horses disappearing overnight, leaving only their metal shoes behind, something crawling inside the rib cage of a cow and eating it from the inside out—these may sound like spooky farmyard stories, but they're actually true tales about the Tasmanian devil dating back to early Tasmanian settlements. Devils have very strong jaws that allow them to crush bones, which means they can even devour an entire carcass!

DINGO VS TASMANIAN TIGER

I AM THE GREATEST!

YOU 'WERE' THE GREATEST.

Who would win in a battle between these fierce fighters? The now-extinct Tasmanian tiger had a more powerful bite than the dingo, but the dingo has stronger head and neck muscles. The end result is anyone's guess!

MYSTERIES

Who killed the swift parrots in Tasmania? Shockingly, their corpses were discovered beheaded in their hollows. Detectives were baffled—until a camera caught the killer in action! It turned out to be the little sugar glider, which usually only eats insects. Talk about an unusual suspect!

YOU TRY EATING INSECTS EVERY DAY!

WHAT KILLER KILLED A KILLER SHARK?

Several years ago, a great white shark was fitted with an electronic tracking tag. Less than three months later, the tag was found washed up on a beach—and what it revealed startled researchers. The shark had been eaten alive! What sort of sea creature could have killed a 10-foot (3-meter)-long shark? Still an unsolved mystery, it might have been a giant squid or a pack of killer whales.

I DID ORDER FISH THAT NIGHT... BUT I DIDN'T GET ANY CHIPS!

I PLEAD NOT GUILTY!

ISN'T THAT A PIECE OF SHARK MEAT UNDER YOUR TONGUE?

Cryptozoology is the study of animals whose existence hasn't been proven. There's the Loch Ness Monster and Big Foot. Big Foot has been around for generations, also known as the "*Sasquatch.*" Scientists discount the existence of Bigfoot and consider it to be a combination of folklore, misidentification, and hoax, rather than a living animal, because of the lack of physical evidence and the large numbers of creatures that would be necessary to maintain a breeding population. Occasional new reports of sightings sustain a small group of self-described investigators.

THE 'WOOD DEVIL'

An illustration and quote from an 1895 book that describes a huge bipedal "wood devil" in northern Queensland.

"He said it was as tall as a man, and walked about on its hind legs, it had long arms and huge hands, and made a strange moaning noise."

BIG FOOT XING

DUE TO SIGHTINGS IN THE AREA OF A CREATURE RESEMBLING "BIG FOOT" THIS SIGN HAS BEEN POSTED FOR YOUR SAFETY

BELIEVE IT OR NOT!

I THOUGHT I SAW A BIG PUDDY CAT

Is there a mysterious panther-like creature slinking secretly around the Australian wilderness? Sightings and reports have been made in both New South Wales and Victoria. So far, investigations haven't been able to find any solid proof of these elusive felines.

HAVE YOU SEEN THE THYLACINE?

In 1936, the thylacine—also known as the Tasmanian tiger—was declared extinct. Even so, there have been hundreds of reported sightings since that time. Most are in northern Tasmania, in areas of suitable habitat. These sightings offer hope that the thylacine isn't extinct after all.

FOOTPRINTS OF THE THYLACINE

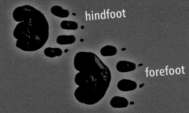

hindfoot

forefoot

CHAPTER 8

BACK FROM THE DEAD

MISSING FOR 36 YEARS. A fencing contractor in central Queensland was flicking through a magazine and saw a picture of the bridled nailtail wallaby, which was believed to be extinct. Fortunately, the sharp-eyed man realized he'd actually just seen one! He reported his suspicions to the Queensland Parks Service, who bought the property in an attempt to protect the wallaby's habitat—just in time!

WHAT'S BROWN AND STICKY?

MISSING FOR 40 YEARS. In 1918, a shipwreck on Lord Howe Island resulted in a swarm of black rats rushing onto the island. The rats promptly gobbled up all the Lord Howe Island stick insects, and by 1920 the species was declared extinct. In 1964, a dead stick insect was discovered on a nearby volcanic rock. Researchers eventually found four live stick insects and have since managed to breed them.

BEATING THE ODDS

MISSING FOR 50 YEARS. Leadbeater's possum was presumed extinct after not being seen for half a century. A single possum was found in Victoria 1961, and it was declared the state's faunal emblem in 1968. Sadly, much of their habitat was destroyed in the 2009 Black Saturday bushfires, and they may soon become endangered.

TINY BUT TENACIOUS

MISSING FOR 100 YEARS. When the mountain pygmy possum was first described from a fossil in 1896, it was already believed to be extinct. A single living specimen was discovered in a ski lodge on Mount Hotham in 1966 and listed in the *Guinness Book of Records* the next year as the rarest animal on Earth!

OUTFOXED

MISSING FOR 100 YEARS. After being declared missing for almost a century, the desert rat kangaroo was rediscovered in 1931, but only for a few short years. It disappeared again in 1935, after having its habitat invaded by red foxes. There goes the neighborhood!

FEATHERING THEIR NEST

SHHH...DON'T TELL ANYONE.

MISSING FOR 170 YEARS. Is there really such a thing as an Australian night parrot? Supposedly discovered in 1845, it's rarely been seen since. After 15 years of searching, a wildlife photographer took several photos and a short video of the bird in western Queensland in 2013. But in order to protect the bird, he's keeping the location top secret!

CLONING EXTINCT ANIMALS

It's no longer science fiction. Scientists haven't quite managed to clone dinosaurs like in the movie *Jurassic Park*—but they're getting closer! Experiments are taking place to clone the woolly mammoth, thylacine and gastric brooding frog. Who knows where this might lead!

As dead as a dodo? Maybe not!

MAMMOTH TASK

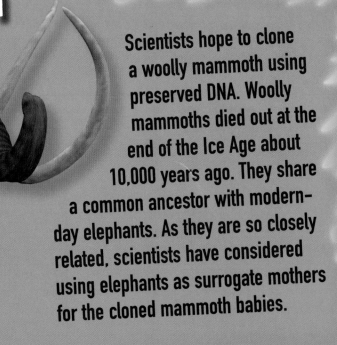

Scientists hope to clone a woolly mammoth using preserved DNA. Woolly mammoths died out at the end of the Ice Age about 10,000 years ago. They share a common ancestor with modern-day elephants. As they are so closely related, scientists have considered using elephants as surrogate mothers for the cloned mammoth babies.

QUITE A MOUTHFUL

NO WONDER I WENT EXTINCT!

Imagine a creature that gives birth through its mouth! The gastric brooding frog would swallow her fertilized eggs and keep them in her stomach until they emerged as fully formed froglets. The species disappeared in the 1980s, and scientists are now trying to revive it. They placed gastric brooding frog nuclei into the eggs of living frogs that had their own genetic material removed and now have embryos of the extinct animal.

EXTINCT ANIMAL CLONE RECIPE

Instant clone — just add DNA!.

INGREDIENTS
- cells from the animal you want to clone

- a related living animal

- sophisticated laboratory equipment

METHOD

1 RECONSTRUCT THE GENOME: Using the genome of the living animal as a guide, reassemble the extinct animal's DNA.

2 SWAP: Remove eggs from the living animal. Replace their nuclei with the extinct animal's restored genetic material.

3 TREAT THE EGGS: Use electric shocks or chemicals to fuse the reconstructed eggs with the nuclei. Wait for cell division to begin.

4 IMPLANT THE NEW EMBRYOS: When the embryos have grown sufficiently, place them in the living animal's uterus.

5 SAVE A SPECIES: Watch as the living animal gives birth to an extinct species!

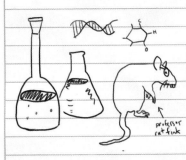

professor rat fink

CHAPTER 9

SPOOKY PLACES

How would you like to live in a cave? It may seem spooky to us, but it's the only place that some animals can call home!

TROGLOXENES

Some animals seek shelter in caves but leave to hunt for food. They're known as trogloxenes. They include bats, birds, moths, crickets and grasshoppers.

LIVING IN A CAVE IS DRIVING ME BATTY!

TROGLOBITES

Other animals spend their whole lives in caves and never leave! They're known as troglobites. They include the cave shrimp and blind salamander. Because they live in a pitch-black world, they have no eyes. They also don't have any color—what would be the point?

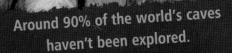
Around 90% of the world's caves haven't been explored.

Cave cricket

STICKY FINGERS

Giant cave geckos come out from their caves at night to hunt for food. They're more active in showery weather, and grow to about 7 inches (18 centimeters) long. Like all geckos, they have sticky plates under their feet to help them stick on to things.

SPOOKY SHIPWRECKS

More than 8,000 ships have sunk off the Australian coastline. Off Victoria's southwest lies one of the most treacherous stretches. Known as the Shipwreck Coast, it's been the final resting place of more than 80 ships!

I WONDER WHY THEY SINK THEIR BOATS?

SUNKEN LOUNGE ROOM

The remains of sunken ships eventually become homes for marine life. Fish make themselves comfortable pretty quickly. Coral also begins to grow over the ship's surface—although this is a much slower process. After many years, it can be difficult to tell the difference between natural marine habitats and those that used to be ships.

OPENING PANDORA'S BOX

The HMS *Bounty* is famous for the mutiny against its captain William Bligh. In November 1790, the HMS *Pandora* was sent to search for the *Bounty* and its crew. The *Pandora* hit a reef in the northern reaches of the Great Barrier Reef. Damaged beyond repair, the ship sank and 35 people on board died. The cause of the wreck is now known as Pandora's Reef, after its ill-fated namesake.

AAARGH! A GHOST!

SIGHTINGS
OF A GHOST SHIP

The SS *Yongala* was a luxury passenger ferry. Lost during a cyclone in 1911, the steamship sank on its journey from Melbourne to Cairns. All 122 on board died—and it is still considered one of Australia's worst maritime disasters. There are rumors of mysterious sightings of a ghost ship in the area matching the *Yongala*'s description. Keep an eye out for it, if you're ever sailing between Bowen and Townsville ...

GHASTLY
GRAVEYARDS

Cemeteries are not just for the dearly departed—they are also home to various types of wildlife. These locations provide everything an animal needs, such as food, water and shelter. Not to mention the neighbors are deathly silent!

CREEPY
COBWEBS

A cemetery near Grafton in New South Wales becomes eerily covered with spiderwebs at certain times of the year. And no, it's not Halloween! The spooky spinning happens during flooding, when spiders set their webs higher up to escape the rising water.

I HAVE GRAVE CONCERNS ABOUT LIVING HERE...

THE EERIE CALL OF THE CURLEW

The haunting sound a curlew makes at night has resulted in people associating them with ghosts.

MARBLED STATUES

The Melbourne Cemetery is home to a huge population of marbled geckos. Like other geckos, they don't have eyelids and clean their eyes with their tongues. You'll probably never see a marbled gecko because the geckos are nocturnal. Blink and you'll miss one!

GRAVEYARD VANDALS

Groups of fearless vandals have moved into some cemeteries. With brazen disregard, they dig holes under the grave covers. They even sunbake on the dark grey slabs! Though there's no point trying to arrest them. These goannas are just doing what comes naturally!

THAT'S SCARY!

GLOSSARY

amateur	a person who does something for enjoyment and does not earn money from it
beheaded	when something has had its head cut off
carcass	the dead body of an animal
companion	a friend
confined space	a place where someone feels cramped and where there may be little fresh air
constrict	to make something tighter or narrower
corpse	a dead body, usually human
decaying	when something is rotting and goes bad
devour	to eat or swallow something quickly and greedily, like a hungry wild animal would
disregard	to treat something without any respect or consideration
emblem	something made to be a sign or symbol
formidable	something that causes fear and dread
gland	a part of the body that makes substances that are then used in other parts of the body
hibernate	when an animal sleeps in a safe place through the winter
hypnotize	to put someone or something in a sleep-like condition and then be able to control their mind and actions

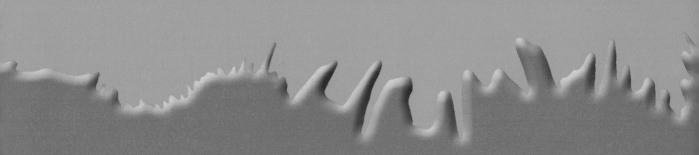

incisor   a tooth used for biting or cutting

interlocking   when things fit into each other so that the parts work well together

lethal   something that can cause death

migrate   to move from one area and settle in another area to live

plankton   a mass of very small animals and plants that drift on or near the surface of the water

provoke   to stir up or anger something, causing it to react

reputation   the way people think of someone or something

scuttle   to run with quick, hurried steps

slough off   to shed or cast off something, such as a snake's skin

submerged   when something is under the surface of the water

taxidermist   someone who prepares, stuffs and mounts the skins of animals so they look alive

toxin   a poison that can cause sickness and even death

treacherous   something risky and dangerous

venomous   a creature, such as a snake or spider, that can inject its poison into a victim

Additional images:

Kathie Atkinson/AUSCAPE: p. 11 (zebra finch caught in web of golden orb-weaver spider); Robert Batty: p. 42 (HMS *Pandora*), *HMS* Pandora *in the act of foundering 29 August 1791*, from a painting by Peter Heywood, 1831; Arthur Bicknall: p. 34 (wood devil engraving) from *Travels and Adventure in Northern Queensland*, 1895, London and New York: Longmans, Green and Co.; Michael Coghlan: p. 27 (diprotodon skull) *Australian Dinosaur Skull*/CC BY-SA 2.0, http://commons.wikimedia.org/wiki/File:Diprotodon_skull.jpg; Carmen Fabro: p. 10 (spider eating bat); John Gould: p. 37 (desert rat kangaroo); Greg Harm: pp. 27 (eastern cave bat skull), 36 (bridled nailtail wallaby) & 42 (Twelve Apostles shrouded in mist); Michael Morcombe: p. 20 (masked lapwing); Ian Morris: pp. 15 (common death adders), 16 (man holding file snake) & 25 (giant centipede eating snake); NAA: p. 31 (Tasmanian tiger) A6180, 21/8/78/15; NLA: p. 34 (article) 'Hairy Man.' *Mudgee Guardian and North-Western Representative* (NSW : 1890 - 1954) 17 Jun 1909: 4. Web. 27 Feb 2015 http://nla.gov.au/nla.news-page16248488; NLA/Neville William Cayley: p. 37 (night parakeet) an6952739; NLA/William Hodges: p. 38 (dodo and red parakeet) an2256824; Polev1979: p. 35 (thylacine) *Tasmanian tiger*/CC BY-SA 3.0, http://commons.wikimedia.org/wiki/File:THYLACINE.jpg; Queensland Museum/Robert Allen: p. 30 (marsupial lion illustration); Queensland Museum/Jeff Wright: p. 5 (Gould's wattled bat); Rushenb: p. 9 (male and female golden orb spider) *Mating spiders, Nephila pilipes – Golden Orb-web Spider*/CC BY 2.0, http://commons.wikimedia.org/wiki/File:Mating_nephila_pilipes_-_golden_orb-web_spider.jpg; State Library of Victoria/Charles Dickson Gregory: p. 43 (S.S. *Yongala*) H96.160/1287; Frederick M. Rossiter: p. 26 (front view of skull) from *The Practical Guide to Health* (Fig. 8), 1910, Mountain View, Cal.: Pacific Press Publishing Association; Ken Stepnell: pp. 4 (wolf spider) & 44 (goanna); Valerie Taylor: pp. 3 & 33 (great white shark), 5 (Maori octopus) & 29 (great white shark with mouth open); Henry Woodward: p. 30 (illustrated skull) *Skull and lower jaw of Thylacoleo carnifex* (Fig. 102) from *A guide to the fossil mammals and birds in the Department of Geology and Palæontology in the British Museum (Natural History)*, 1896.

Text:

p.34 (description of the wood devil) from *Travels and Adventure in Northern Queensland* by Arthur Bicknall, 1895, London and New York: Longmans, Green and Co.

Licences:

http://creativecommons.org/licenses/by/2.0/deed.en
http://creativecommons.org/licenses/by-sa/2.0/deed.en
http://creativecommons.org/licenses/by-sa/3.0/deed.en